Meet NASA Inventor Marco Pavone and His

Leaping Low-Gravity Explorers

WORLD BOOK

www.worldbook.com

World Book, Inc.
180 North LaSalle Street
Suite 900
Chicago, Illinois 60601
USA

For information about other World Book publications, visit our website at www.worldbook.com or call 1-800-WORLDBK (967-5325).

For information about sales to schools and libraries, call 1-800-975-3250 (United States), or 1-800-837-5365 (Canada).

Produced in collaboration with the National Aeronautics and Space Administration (NASA).

Library of Congress Cataloging-in-Publication Data for this volume has been applied for.

Out of This World
ISBN: 978-0-7166-6261-7 (set, hc.)

Leaping Low-Gravity Explorers
ISBN: 978-0-7166-6263-1 (hc.)
ISBN: 978-0-7166-6279-2 (pf.)

Also available as:
ISBN: 978-0-7166-6271-6 (e-book)

Staff

Editorial

Director
Tom Evans

Manager, New Content
Jeff De La Rosa

Writer
William D. Adams

Proofreader/Indexer
Nathalie Strassheim

Graphics and Design

Senior Visual
Communications Designer
Melanie Bender

Media Researcher
Rosalia Bledsoe

Acknowledgments

Cover	© Jurik Peter, Shutterstock; NASA/JPL-Caltech/Stanford
4-5	© Dotted Yeti/Shutterstock
6-7	NASA/JPL
8-13	© Shutterstock
14-15	© Mark Garlick, Science Photo Library/Getty Images
16-17	Marco Pavone; © Lindasky76/Shutterstock
18-19	ESA/CNES/ARIANESPACE-Service Optique CSG, 2004
20-21	© Mikkel Juul Jensen, Science Source
23	NASA
25	Marco Pavone
27	© Africa Studio/Shutterstock
28-29	NASA/JPL-Caltech/Stanford
30-31	© Volodymyr Goinyk, Shutterstock; JAXA
32-33	© Nostalgia for Infinity/Shutterstock
34-35	Marco Pavone; NASA
36-39	Marco Pavone
40-41	Marco Pavone ; NASA/JPL-Caltech
43-44	Marco Pavone

Contents

Glossary There is a glossary of terms on page 45. Terms defined in the glossary are in boldface type that **looks like this** on their first appearance on any spread (two facing pages).

Pronunciations (how to say words) are given in parentheses the first time some difficult words appear in the book. They look like this: pronunciation (pruh NUHN see AY shuhn).

Introduction

Most of us are familiar with the massive, dazzling worlds of our **solar system.** The names Jupiter, Mars, and even the moon summon images of vast, shining orbs and complex alien landscapes. But there is more to our solar system than just moons and planets. In the vast stretches of space that separate these bodies lurk the small and unusual— the **asteroids, comets,** and other crumbs of matter left over from the formation of the rest of the solar system. Together, these objects are known as **small solar system bodies (SSSB's).**

It might be easy to think that SSSB's matter little to our lives and to our understanding of the solar system. But their ranks may include ancient voyagers, water carriers, resource bearers, and planet destroyers. SSSB's have played an important role in the evolution of life on Earth, for example causing asteroid strikes that led to mass extinctions. Many SSSB's are rich in resources, making them tempting targets for space exploration.

To learn more about objects in space, scientists and **engineers** often send **rovers** to explore their surfaces. But **small solar system bodies (SSSB's)** present a unique challenge to rovers—their extremely weak **gravitational pull.** On a massive world like Mars or the moon, gravity holds a rover to the surface. The downward pull of gravity also helps the rover's wheels get traction, enabling it to move around. In the extremely low-gravity environment on an SSSB, a traditional rover would struggle for traction. And, if it **accelerated** too quickly, the rover might go flinging off into space.

Space explorers, however, are working to turn this weakness into an advantage. The same low-gravity environment that makes it hard for rovers to roll actually makes it easier for them to hop. To explore SSSB's effectively, rovers will have to be developed that can leap, and leap with control. Stanford University engineer Marco Pavone (pronounced *pah VOH nay*) is working to build just such a leaping low-gravity explorer.

The rover Sojourner explores Mars. Wheeled rovers are great for rocky planets and large moons, but different designs are needed for SSSB's.

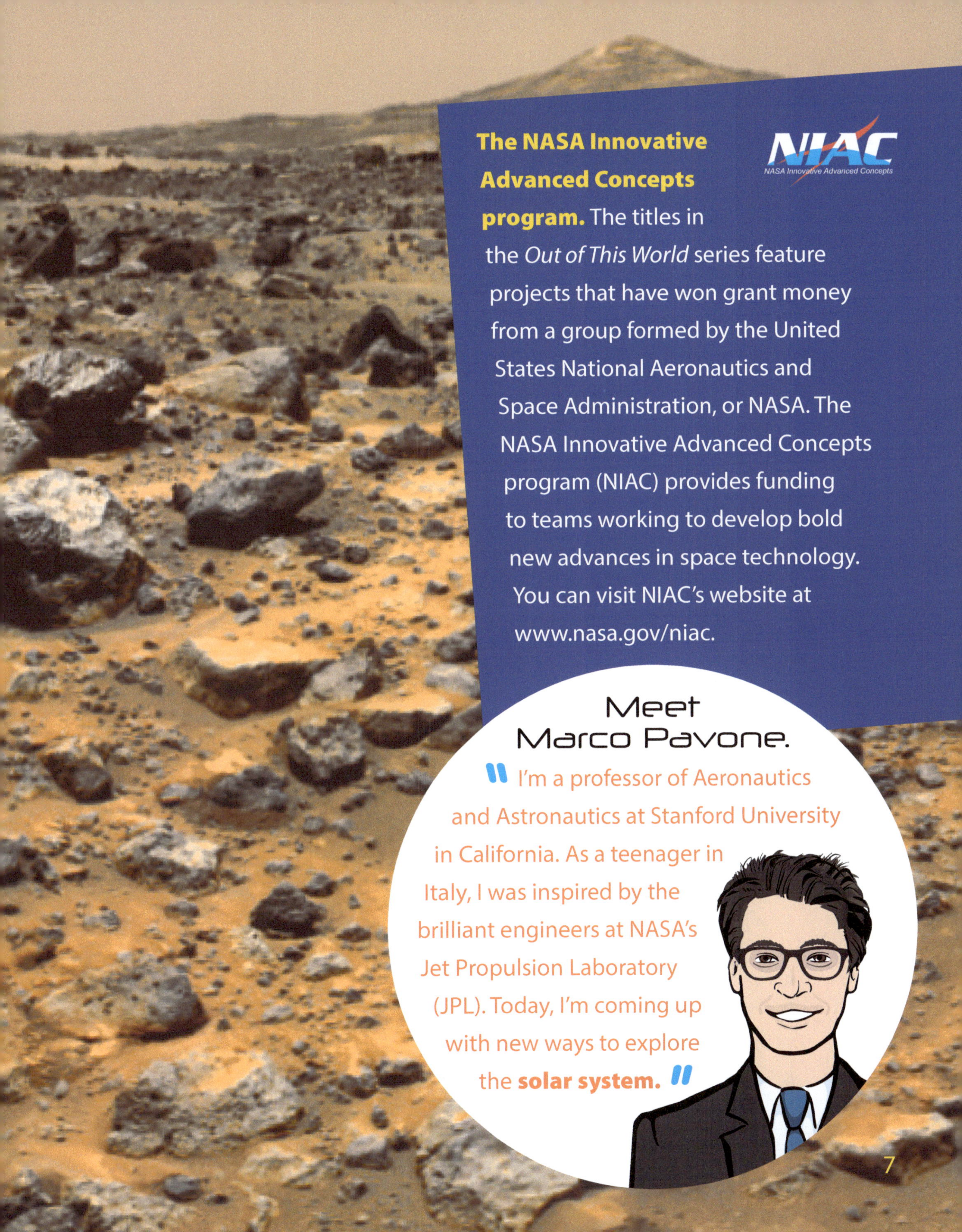

The NASA Innovative Advanced Concepts program. The titles in the *Out of This World* series feature projects that have won grant money from a group formed by the United States National Aeronautics and Space Administration, or NASA. The NASA Innovative Advanced Concepts program (NIAC) provides funding to teams working to develop bold new advances in space technology. You can visit NIAC's website at www.nasa.gov/niac.

Meet Marco Pavone.

" I'm a professor of Aeronautics and Astronautics at Stanford University in California. As a teenager in Italy, I was inspired by the brilliant engineers at NASA's Jet Propulsion Laboratory (JPL). Today, I'm coming up with new ways to explore the **solar system.** "

What are small solar system bodies?

Billions of years ago, our **solar system** formed from a swirling cloud of dust and gas in space. The center of the cloud condensed to become a star, the sun. The rest of the material spun around the forming star. Occasionally, particles of this material collided. The particles combined as they collided, forming bigger and bigger objects.

Every object has a **gravitational pull.** For small objects, this pull is very weak. As an object increases in **mass,** its pull becomes stronger. In this way, the larger objects drew in even more particles. Eventually, some objects became so massive that their gravitational pulls compressed them more or less into spheres. The roughly spherical objects became the planets, **dwarf planets,** and large moons of our solar system. There are over 100 of them.

Objects less than about 600 miles (1,000 kilometers) across were not massive enough to be pulled into spheres. As a result, they have a variety of lumpy shapes. These are the **small solar system bodies.**

Types of small solar system bodies

The International Astronomical Union (IAU), the recognized authority in naming heavenly bodies, has defined a **small solar system body (SSSB)** as any object **orbiting** the sun that is not massive enough to pull itself into a rounded shape. This definition includes most **asteroids, comets,** and small **Kuiper belt objects (KBO's).**

Asteroids are rocky or metallic objects that orbit a star. In our **solar system,** many asteroids are found in the main asteroid belt, between the orbits of Mars and Jupiter. Many others roam other parts of the solar system, however.

Comets are icy bodies that release gas and dust. Most of the comets that can be seen from Earth travel around the sun in long, oval orbits. Once in a while, a comet will come close to the sun, producing a brilliant tail of gas and dust that can be seen from Earth for days or weeks.

Kuiper belt objects are icy bodies
that circle the sun beyond the orbit
of the planet Neptune, in a region
called the **Kuiper belt.** Some KBO's
are large enough to be rounded by
their **gravity,** but most of them are
SSSB's.

The IAU's definition excludes the
solar system's many small moons, as
they orbit planets or other bodies,
rather than the sun. But small moons
have much in common with SSSB's,
and many of them are probably
SSSB's that were captured into orbit
around a larger body. Many scientists
therefore consider small moons and
SSSB's to be fundamentally similar.

Why study small solar system bodies?

Why is it important to study these small, misshapen misfits? Many **asteroids, comets,** and **KBO's** are essentially leftovers from the formation of the **solar system.** They preserve important clues about how the solar system came into being and how it has changed over time.

Small solar system bodies (SSSB's) may have also played an important role in the development of life. Many scientists think that comets or asteroids crashing to Earth brought water and other chemicals important for life to evolve. Studying SSSB's could help us understand if this process could have happened elsewhere in the solar system or even the universe.

SSSB's could serve as stepping stones for exploring the rest of the solar system. A space **probe** could hitch a ride on a comet or asteroid to visit the outer planets. Or a space agency might set up a robotic mining depot on an asteroid. Such a facility could provide important mineral resources or serve as a refueling station for deep-space missions.

Perhaps the most urgent reason to study SSSB's is to defend our planet against them. Occasionally, a comet or asteroid collides with Earth. The results range from minor damage to global disaster, depending mostly on the size of the object. Many scientists suspect, for example, that the collision with a mountain-sized asteroid some 65 million years ago played a major role in the *extinction* (dying out) of the dinosaurs. By studying SSSB's, scientists and **engineers** may come up with ways to deflect them, averting future disaster.

Send rover on over

It is clear that **small solar system bodies (SSSB's)** are important targets for study.

So the question becomes, 'How do you study these bodies?' —Marco

To get up close and personal, mission planners might send a simple **lander.** A lander is a **probe** that touches down on the surface and stays in one place.

It turns out that small bodies, even though they are small, actually present quite a bit of diversity on their surface, in terms of their chemical and physical properties. —Marco

Imagine a group of alien scientists sending a lander to Earth. Because oceans cover 70 percent of the planet, the lander would probably splash down in salt water. But these alien scientists would be wrong to assume that the entire surface is ocean. Even on land, the makeup of Earth's rock—not to mention its plant and animal life—varies greatly from place to place. To get a better understanding of Earth's surface, the aliens would have to send a **rover** to explore a variety of environments. The same is true, on a smaller scale, of SSSB's.

Consider two SSSB's that have been studied by spacecraft: the **comet** 67P/Churyumov-Gerasimenko (by the European probe Rosetta) and the **KBO** Arrokoth (by the NASA probe New Horizons). Each body has two distinct *lobes* (lumps), looking something like a dumbbell or snowman. The lobes were probably separate bodies that became connected. Therefore, each lobe could have a vastly different history and properties. A rover could move between two such lobes, studying both.

**Artist's illustration
of Arrokoth**

Inventor feature:

Early life and education

Pavone was born in Torino (Turin), a city in northern Italy. His father was a judge, which required the family to move to different parts of Italy every four or five years.

Pavone at eight years old

After a while, the family settled in Sicily, a large island south of the Italian mainland, where Pavone attended high school. There, he did not study **engineering** or technology. He studied the *humanities*—such subjects as language, literature, philosophy, and art.

❚❚ Such subjects as Latin and ancient Greek aren't directly applicable to designing spacecraft, but their study helped to *scaffold* [structure] my critical thinking skills and my desire to look deeply at problems. **"** —Marco

Pavone attended college at Sicily's University of Catania and Scuola Superiore of Catania, where he learned the mathematics needed to study engineering.

" My college education provided the mathematical foundation for all I do. Everything I do is written in the language of mathematics, so becoming fluent in that language was extremely important. **"** —Marco

Gravity:
The cause of—and solution to—all of space exploration's problems

One of the biggest obstacles to exploring **small solar system bodies (SSSB's)** is that they lack sufficient **gravitation.** Gravitation, sometimes called the force or pull of gravity, is an attraction between objects because of their **mass.** An object's mass is its amount of matter. In general, the more mass an object has, the stronger the pull it exerts.

A massive object, such as Earth, exerts an incredible gravitational pull. Earth's gravitation holds us to the planet so tightly that it takes an extremely powerful rocket to escape into space. Gravitation is thus a major headache for **engineers** trying to launch a space **probe.**

Once an **orbiter** reaches its destination, however, the opposite can be true. Such probes rely on gravitation to slow them down, pulling them into **orbit** around their intended targets. It's no problem when the target is a massive planet like Mars or Jupiter. But SSSB's have much less mass, resulting in a weaker gravitational pull.

Probes tend to go flinging right by SSSB's. To stick around, a probe must either bring along huge amounts of fuel, blasting its **thrusters** in reverse to slow down, or it must take a long, complicated path to approach its target more slowly.

The European probe Rosetta, for example, took 10 years to reach the **comet** 67P/Churyumov-Gerasimenko. Along the way, Rosetta swung by Earth and Mars, taking advantage of their gravitational pulls to align its path closely with that of the comet. Once there, it still had to fire thrusters to enter orbit around the comet.

Rosetta launches aboard an Ariane 5 rocket on March 2, 2004.

Gravitation does not just enable a **probe** to enter **orbit** around an object. It also helps a probe to land—and stay—on an object's surface.

When we walk or run on Earth, for example, we push against the ground with our feet. As a result, we are pushed upward as well as forward. Earth's gravitational pull counteracts this upward force, keeping us from flying into the air.

SSSB's have much weaker gravitational pulls. On an **asteroid** smaller than about 2.5 miles (4 kilometers) across, for example, a

Illustration of Philae's bouncy landing (not to scale)

simple leap could send an astronaut drifting into space. That may sound like fun, but it makes exploring SSSB's extremely difficult.

The Rosetta mission showed just how difficult it is to land on an SSSB. The probe reached **comet** 67P/Churyumov-Gerasimenko in 2014, carrying a small **lander** called Philae. The comet, less than 3 miles (4.5 kilometers) in diameter at its widest point, had far too weak a gravitational pull to reliably hold a lander to its surface. For this reason, Philae was equipped with harpoons to anchor it to the comet's surface.

The harpoons failed to fire when Philae touched down. The probe rebounded, bouncing to about 0.6 mile (1 kilometer) above the comet's surface. After another bounce, Philae settled in a heavily shaded area. Without sunlight on its solar panels, the craft could not recharge its batteries. It was only able to conduct observations for about 2 $\frac{1}{2}$ days before it ran out of energy.

Some 20 years before the Rosetta mission, Marco Pavone's interest in space was piqued by another mission—the Pathfinder mission to Mars.

Landing on Mars presents its own difficulties. Mars, like Earth, has a strong **gravitational pull,** making it easier for the planet to draw in **orbiters** and **landers.** But unlike Earth, Mars has a very thin **atmosphere,** making it difficult to slow down incoming landers using friction with the air or parachutes.

To safely land Pathfinder, **engineers** enclosed the craft in four huge, connected airbags, similar to those that protect people in automobile accidents. A parachute and simple **retrorockets** would slow the craft somewhat. But they would cut out many feet or meters above the ground as the airbags inflated.

Pathfinder reached Mars in 1997. It hit the surface at about 30 miles (50 kilometers) per hour and bounced at least 15 times before coming to rest. The landing—along with the rest of the mission—was a stunning success. The lander released a small wheeled **rover** named Sojourner that explored the **terrain** nearby.

Engineers test the airbag system used to land Mars Pathfinder.

Marco was in high school when Pathfinder landed. Hearing about the mission inspired him to become an engineer.

> I didn't know the names of the engineers who developed the landing system and other parts of the mission, but they became heroes to me. I wanted to be like them when I grew up, tackling complex challenges in novel ways. —Marco

After graduating the University of Catania and the Scuola Superiore of Catania, Marco Pavone moved to the United States to pursue a Ph.D. in Aeronautics and Astronautics at the Massachusetts Institute of Technology.

Slipping and sliding

A wheeled **rover** like Sojourner would not work well on a **small solar system body (SSSB)** because of the low-**gravity** environment. Think about automobiles driving in icy conditions. Lighter automobiles tend to slide more easily in such conditions. To counteract this tendency, car owners will sometimes try to put additional weight over the wheels, for example placing sandbags in an automobile's trunk. The idea is that the added downward force helps to improve the wheels' traction.

On an SSSB, the gravitational pull is simply not strong enough to provide much downward force. A wheeled rover would thus struggle to gain traction.

" In such a low-gravity environment, wheels would not work well. Wheels require traction and traction requires gravity. And since we don't have much gravity, the wheels would just spin in place. **"** —Marco

If the rover did manage to gain traction, it would likely push off the surface and tumble in the low-gravity conditions. These problems led Pavone to a novel approach.

" Traditionally, mission planners have seen the lack of gravity as an obstacle to be overcome. Instead, why don't we try to take advantage of the lack of gravity, with a novel way of moving tailored to the low-gravity conditions? **"** —Marco

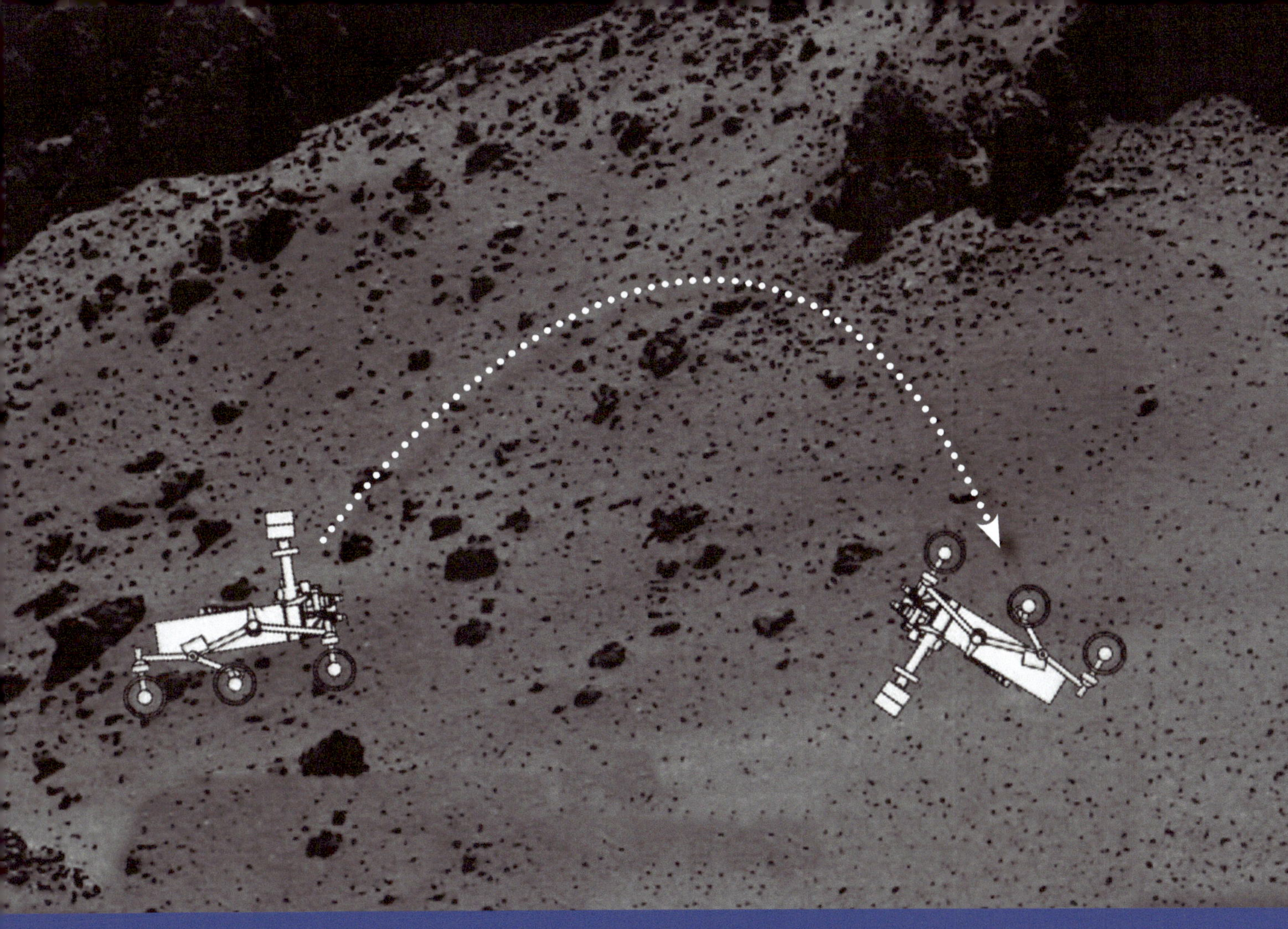

A rover that hopped, instead of rolling, might maneuver more effectively in a low-gravity environment. But how to make the craft hop? Using **thrusters** would require fuel in the form of **propellant,** making the rover heavier and more expensive. And a system involving springs or some other external mechanism might struggle to operate on the rugged, dusty surface of an SSSB.

On an SSSB, a wheeled probe would struggle to gain traction. If it did, it would likely push off the surface and flip over.

Big idea:
Internal actuation

Actuation refers to movement. In robotics, *actuators* are such devices as motors that cause parts of the robot to move. Normally, actuators would be mounted on the outside of a rover. But in 2010, Pavone and fellow JPL **engineer** Issa Nesnas thought it might be a good idea to put the actuators inside a rover—internal actuation.

To accomplish this feat, the two turned to a device called the **flywheel.** A flywheel is a heavy disc attached to a motor. In their design, the motor spins the flywheel up to high speed. The spinning flywheel has **momentum.** If a brake is suddenly applied, that momentum is instantly transferred to the braking device—and in this case, to the rover. In essence, stopping the heavy flywheel causes the craft to jerk in one direction.

A hamster can explore a house in a hamster ball while being protected from most dangers. The hamster moves the ball from the inside in an example of internal actuation.

Flywheels are not used for actuation on Earth—the amount of momentum transferred is usually not enough to create much movement. But in a low-gravity environment, even a relatively gentle jerk can send a **probe** bounding across an SSSB's surface.

Enter the Hedgehog

Pavone and Nesnas came up with the idea for a hopping, cube-shaped **rover** called Hedgehog. The rover has no top or bottom. Rather it is designed to tumble, something like the dice used to play board games. The rover can function the same no matter which of its six sides it lands on. Each side will be equipped with cameras and other instruments.

A single **flywheel** mechanism can only move a rover in one direction on its own. So Hedgehog has three flywheels positioned at right angles to one another. No matter which side the **probe** lands on, one flywheel will always be parallel to the ground. Two will be perpendicular to the ground. Hedgehog will use small movements of its parallel flywheel to twist itself around. Then, it can activate one of its perpendicular flywheels to hop in the direction it needs to go.

Hedgehog still needs some traction to keep itself from sliding and skidding across the surface of a **small solar system body (SSSB).** This traction is provided by eight knobs sticking out from its corners. Four of these knobs contact the surface when the rover is at rest.

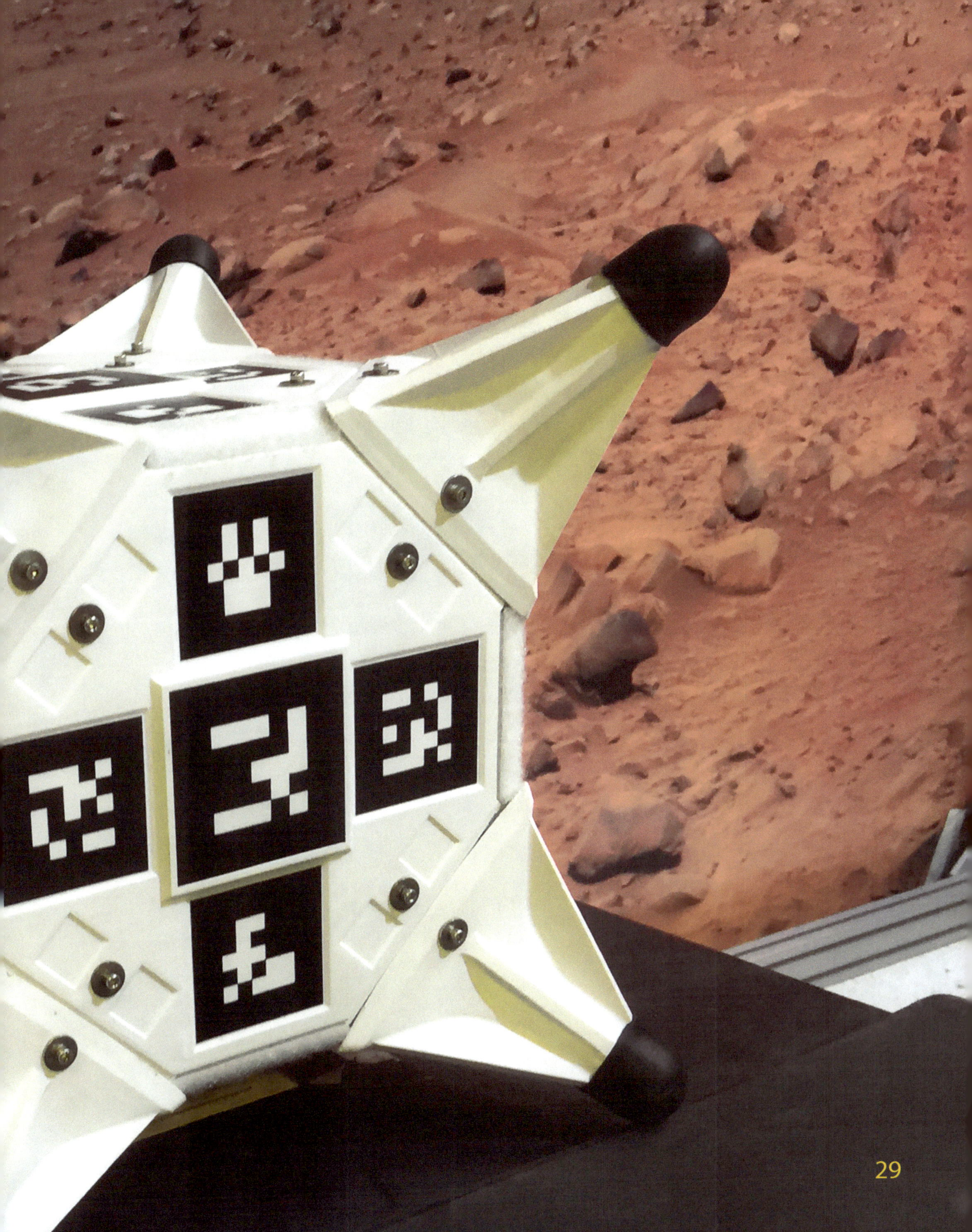

Other benefits of flywheels

Hedgehog has another advantage over **rovers** with wheels or other external mechanisms. The **flywheels** and all other moving parts and sensitive electronics are sealed inside Hedgehog's cubic body, protecting them from such hazards as dust, extreme temperatures, and **radiation.**

Dust. **Small solar system bodies (SSSB's)** are constantly bombarded by tiny bits of rock and other matter floating in space. Over billions of years, such bombardment can pulverize the surface into a layer of powdery dust. This dust can get inside motors and other moving parts, causing them to break down.

Extreme temperatures. An SSSB in the inner **solar system** can easily become broiling hot on its sun-facing side and bitterly cold in shaded regions. Hedgehog's insulated body can keep sensitive parts within a safe temperature range without much need for power-hungry heaters or radiators.

Radiation. The sun gives off high-energy radiation that can damage a spacecraft's electronics. Hedgehog's compact design will enable its sensitive parts to be better protected from such damage.

The first hoppers

In 2018, the Japanese Hyabusa2 mission landed two rovers on the **asteroid** Ryugu. The rovers, named MINERVA-II-1a and MINERVA-II-1b, used a similar **internal actuation** concept to hop across the surface. The mission showed that flywheel-powered hoppers can work. But the Japanese rovers lacked the precision control the Hedgehog rover is designed to provide.

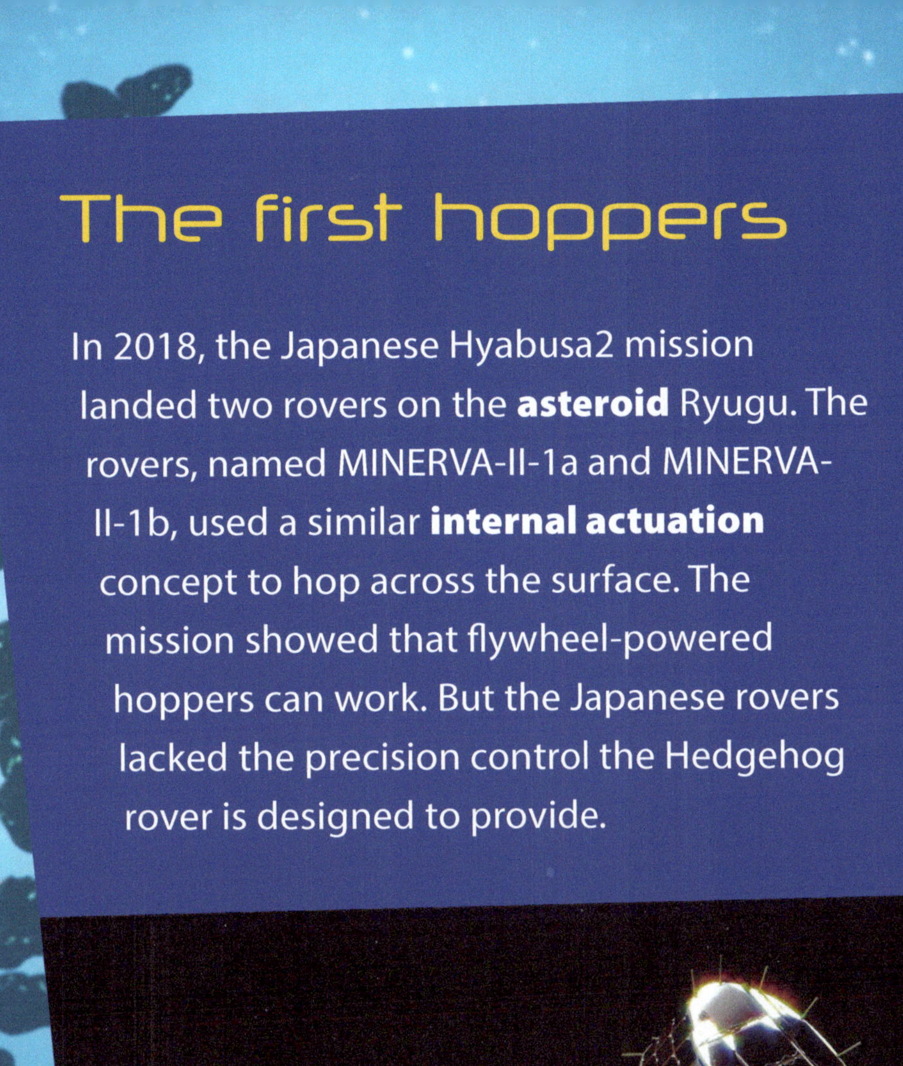

Crazy golf

Even with three **flywheels,** maneuvering Hedgehog with precision on the surface of a **small solar system body (SSSB)** will not be easy.

Mission planners would have to scan the terrain, predict how various areas will react when the **rover** hits them, and plan its path accordingly.

An object's gravitational pull is not the same across its entire surface. Variations in the object's shape and density cause certain spots to experience slightly more or less gravitation. On Earth, with its relatively strong gravitational pull, such variations are too small to notice. But on an SSSB, the overall gravitation is much weaker, making variations far more noticeable. And because SSSB's have such lumpy shapes, even the direction of gravity can vary significantly from place to place.

Just like Earth, an SSSB rotates around its axis. This rotation, combined with an SSSB's weak gravitation, could cause the rover to bounce quite unpredictably. And, in the weaker gravitational pull, such bounces could take hours.

Testing the Hedgehog

To see if Hedgehog will work as planned, Pavone had to test the **rover** in low-gravity conditions. On Earth, such conditions can only be simulated.

❚❚ First, we built a special test bed whereby, using a powered gantry system, we removed almost all the **gravity** from a Hedgehog **prototype.** ❚❚ —Marco

In the test bed, the prototype Hedgehog is held by devices called *gimbals,* which enable the craft to rotate freely. The gimbals in turn hang by cable from a *gantry* (mobile framework). **Sensors** track the forces exerted by the gimbals and feed the information to motors that move the gantry, simulating reduced gravity.

Illustration of a Hedgehog prototype in the low-gravity test bed

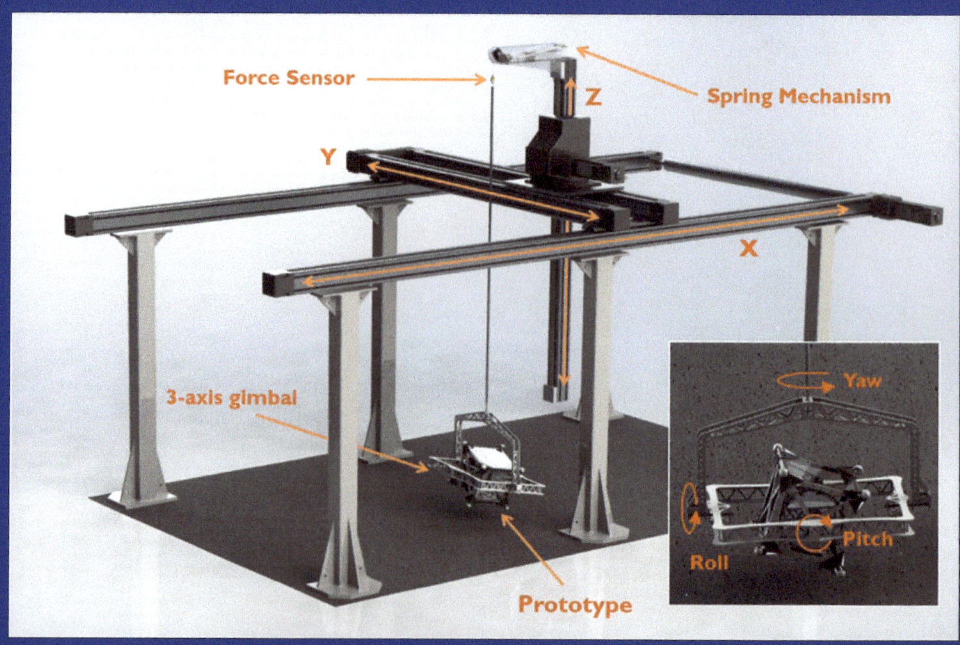

The test bed helped to prove that Hedgehog works. But it has many limitations. For one example, it could only apply low-gravity conditions to the rover, not to the material it is bouncing on.

❚❚ It is not just the rover that acts differently in low-gravity conditions, but also the dust and other surface materials. To test both the robot and the surface material in realistic gravity conditions, we also performed parabolic flight experiments. ❚❚ —Marco

Such experiments are conducted in a special airplane, which alternately climbs and drops in a humplike path called a *parabola*. During the steep dives, the plane's crew and cargo experience reduced gravity conditions.

Vomit Comet

Various parabolic test aircraft have been nicknamed "Vomit Comet" for the queasiness their flight paths can induce in passengers.

Pavone's interest in exploration is not just professional. In his personal time, he enjoys hiking, skiing, scuba diving, and exploring the outdoors.

" I like extreme environments. I don't like flat. I don't like running. I don't like jogging. I'd rather find myself on a mountain or underwater. " —Marco

Pavone has been diving since he was 14. He loves exploring coral reefs, shipwrecks, and underwater caves.

" It's the closest you can get to being in space. " —Marco

Participating in the parabolic flight testing of Hedgehog offered Pavone the opportunity of a lifetime. While testing the **prototype,** he also got to experience the sensation of weightlessness provided by the plane's steep dives.

❝ It was one of the best experiences of my life… not to be bound by any forces; being able to do whatever I wanted. That was very cool! **❞** —Marco

Marco also plays classical guitar.

❝ It's a great way to relax. **❞** —Marco

Mission to Phobos

One intriguing destination for Pavone's leaping low-gravity explorers might be Mars's moon Phobos. Mars has two moons—Phobos and Deimos. They are not large and round like Earth's moon. Instead, they are tiny, lumpy bodies just a few miles or kilometers across.

Astronomers are unsure how these bodies formed. They could be **asteroids** that wandered too close to Mars and were pulled into **orbit** by the planet's **gravitational pull.** But most studies suggest they are leftovers from a huge collision between Mars and another body billions of years ago.

The exploration of Phobos would likely begin with an uncrewed visit, for example landing multiple Hedgehog **rovers** on the surface. These rovers would transmit data to a satellite orbiting Phobos, which would then relay them back to Earth.

On average, it takes nearly 14 minutes for radio signals from Mars to reach Earth and vice versa. This fact makes it extremely difficult for pilots on Earth to control Mars craft directly. Imagine a Hedgehog

was headed toward a dangerous obstacle. It would take nearly half
an hour for this information to reach Earth and for controllers to
transmit a course correction.

As a result, Pavone and his team are working to make Hedgehog
somewhat *autonomous*. **Autonomy** is the degree to which a robot
can make decisions without help from a human operator. Hedgehog
must be able to make decisions on how best to activate its flywheels
to reach a target set by mission controllers on Earth.

Anatomy of a Hedgehog

Like robotic dice, Hedgehog rovers will tumble across **small solar system bodies (SSSB's),** recording data from multiple points on the surface.

Three flywheel-brake assemblies allow the Hedgehog to hop and maneuver in any direction.

Sensor groups on the other three faces will enable the Hedgehog to view and record other data on its surroundings.

Two battery packs will power the rover. There's not enough space for solar panels, so the rover would work until its batteries ran out.

Eight knobby contact points will keep the Hedgehog steady regardless of its orientation or the terrain.

What's in a name?

At first, Pavone and his team thought the best way to gain traction on the craggy surface of an SSSB was to cover the rover with long spikes. This made the probe look a bit like a curled-up hedgehog. Later simulations showed that eight knobs—one at each corner—was a better design. But by that time, the name Hedgehog had stuck!

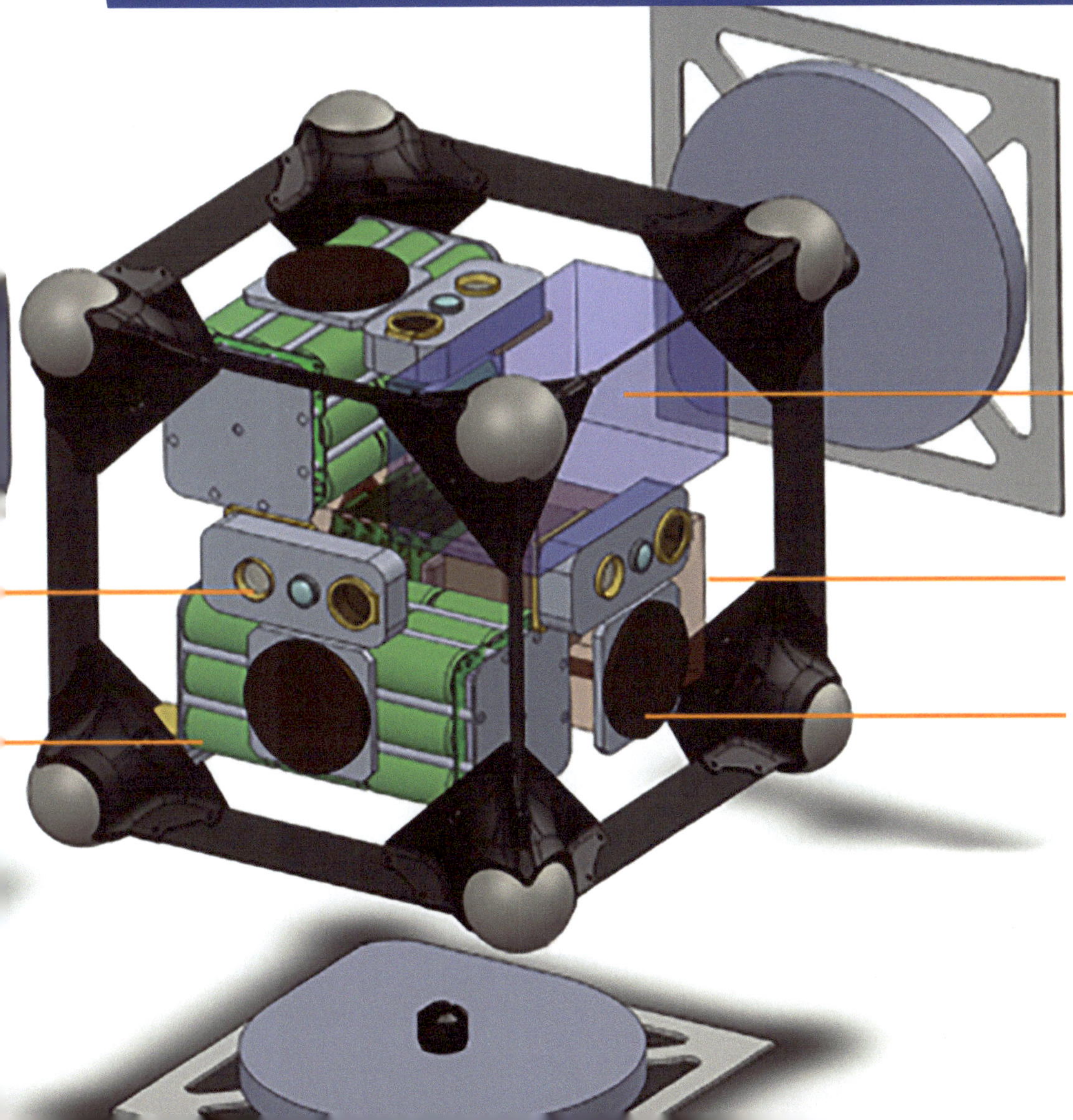

Pavone and his team have saved space on the Hedgehog for scientific instruments.

The Hedgehog's computer will guide it autonomously.

Three antennas will connect each Hedgehog with its orbiting mother satellite and other nearby Hedgehogs.

At Stanford University, Pavone teaches classes on robotics and **autonomy.** He is also the director of a research group called the Autonomous Systems Lab (ASL).

" As a faculty member, you tend to have a lot of ideas, but you do not have time to work on all of them. **"** —Marco

The ASL helps him develop many ideas at once. Scientists, **engineers,** and students at many levels work with Pavone on his projects. He, in turn, helps to advance their academic careers.

One ASL project is a special robotic gripper to be used in space. Many pieces of space technology were not designed to be grasped. And, in near-weightless conditions, one wrong bump could send the gripper and its target careening away from each other.

Pavone teamed up with engineer and fellow Stanford professor Mark Cutkosky to design a sticky gripper, similar to the pads on a gecko's feet. A robot with such a gripper might be able to clear dangerous debris, build structures, or stick to and repair satellites in **orbit.**

Pavone and his team are also interested in how autonomous vehicles *navigate* (map out how they will get to a destination) and make decisions. Some of this work may be helpful in designing an autonomous guidance system for Hedgehog **rovers.** Similarly, some of the technology developed to guide Hedgehog might one day be used in self-driving cars.

Marco Pavone and his team

Marco Pavone and Stanford University's Autonomous Systems Laboratory

Glossary

accelerate to change speed, to speed up.

asteroid a rocky or metallic body smaller than a planet that orbits the sun.

atmosphere the mass of gases that surrounds a planet.

autonomy the degree to which a robot can make decisions without help from a human operator to achieve a goal.

comet an icy body that releases gas or dust.

dwarf planet a rounded body orbiting the sun that does not have enough gravitational pull to clear other objects from its orbit.

engineer a person who uses scientific principles to design structures, such as bridges and skyscrapers, machines, and all sorts of products.

flywheel a heavy, spinning disc attached to a motor.

gravitation also called gravitational pull or force of gravity, the force of attraction that acts between all objects because of their mass. Because of gravitation, an object that is near Earth falls toward the surface of the planet. We experience this force on our bodies as our weight.

internal actuation movement provided by devices enclosed inside the body of a robot, for example the flywheels used by Hedgehog.

Kuiper belt a region of icy objects in the outer solar system, beginning around the orbit of the planet Neptune. The Kuiper belt is also called the Edgeworth-Kuiper belt or the trans-Neptunian disk. An Irish scientist named Kenneth E. Edgeworth suggested in 1943 that the belt existed. The Dutch-born American astronomer Gerard P. Kuiper described it in more detail in 1951.

Kuiper belt object (KBO) any of the icy objects found in the Kuiper belt.

lander a spacecraft designed to land on a planet, moon, or other body in space.

mass the amount of matter something contains.

momentum an object's force of motion. The momentum of a moving object equals its mass multiplied by its *velocity* (speed in a given direction).

orbit a looping path around an object in space; the condition of circling a massive object in space under the influence of the object's gravity.

orbiter a spacecraft designed to orbit a planet or other object in space.

probe a rocket, satellite, or other unmanned spacecraft carrying scientific instruments, to record or report back information about space.

propellant solid or liquid fuel that is turned into gas and put under pressure to push a spacecraft forward.

prototype a functional experimental model of an invention.

radiation energy given off in the form of waves or tiny particles of matter.

retrorocket reverse-firing rockets used to slow and steer spacecraft.

rover a lander designed to move about for surface exploration.

sensor a device that detects heat, light, or some other phenomenon, producing an electric signal.

small solar system body (SSSB) an object in the solar system that does not have enough mass to pull itself into a rounded shape.

solar system the sun and everything that travels around it, including Earth and all the other planets and their moons.

terrain an area of land, usually used when referring to the land's surface natural features.

thruster a rocket or other device used to help steer and control the motion of a spacecraft.

Inventor challenge:
Internal actuation

Marco Pavone's Hedgehog uses internal actuation to prevent dust from damaging its components. Can you think of another use for this idea? Design a new rover that uses internal actuation.

STEP 1

Think about the challenge

Research some extreme environments in the solar system. Include other solar system bodies and extreme environments of Earth itself. Think about what scientists want to learn about these environments. How could a rover using internal actuation help study them while being protected from some of their hazards?

STEP 2

Create your prototype

Pick one of the extreme environments you researched and design a rover that uses internal actuation to explore it. How will your rover move around? How will it study the environment? Will it rely entirely on internal actuation, or will there be external components as well?

STEP 3

Share your design

Remember how Pavone performed physical tests and computer simulations to prove his Hedgehog concept. Develop a plan to test your prototype. If possible, share your design and testing plan with engineers and scientists.

STEP 4

Grow your idea

See if you can make a simple vehicle that uses internal actuation to experiment with the concept. For example, put a small remote-controlled car in a large hamster ball. Aside from having fun, you might discover something that leads you to revise your prototype or testing plan.

Index